Backstories

Poems

Maryfrances Wagner

Published by Spartan Press

Spartan
Press

Cover design and layout: Greg Field

ISBN 978-1-958182-94-9

LCCN 2024946200

Also by Maryfrances Wagner

Solving for X
The Silence of Red Glass
The Immigrants' New Camera
Dioramas
Pouf
Red Silk
Light Subtracts Itself
Salvatore's Daughter

Praise for *Backstories*

Maryfrances Wagner pulls no punches in her brilliant book of poems *Backstories*, where she presents the joy, the fulfillment, and the fraught nature of classroom teaching, where students are learning to live and sometimes just let live. From the mischief of the teacher locked inside a classroom closet and finally released by a student at the end of class, to the painful results of simply allowing a student to use the restroom where he beats another student senseless, these poems reveal how students survive, or not. Of course, there are tranquil times, but in the gritty moments, teachers and students often hold onto each other with hope. The book is a tour-de-force of authenticity where empathy and kindness await their moment while facing the harsh realities of human behavior. But amid the abundance of personal tragedy, I could not stop laughing while reading "Sophomores Study Grammar" when a student asks, "We never stop learning in here, do we? Is it too late to drop this class?" *Backstories* should be required reading for all of us – teachers, parents, students, and school administrators. And what's left after a lifetime of teaching? Attending a centennial, alumni gathering, Maryfrances writes, "I raise someone's pom-poms and sing."

—Walter Bargen, First Missouri Poet Laureate, *Orwell at the Kremlin*

The "backstory" of this book's title for me chronicles teachers who stayed, who came back each day, did not give up on sophomores who "Crunch ice, suck candies, / smack, blow bubbles," or those who ask, "How will I use this in real life?" Here, roaming hands of sweethearts go with new retainers. Eric drove off a cliff into that good night; but if you are left hopeless, don't read this book of hope. It's coming for you, infused with the teacher who sews up a rip in a student's sweater, like a meditation: "Perfect imperfection. / Lives held still in our hands." Observe poems floating in the rarified globe of detention, where students talk; a teacher listens: Holly, whose "mother said even a perfect child can burn / down a house whatever that means." Those lives—the high achiever, the boy clicking his tongue stud against his teeth, the girl out a year to have her baby—each suddenly, in the poems of Maryfrances Wagner, made beautiful.

—Robert Stewart, *Higher* and *Working Class* poems.

Praise for *Backstories*

Maryfrances Wagner, poet, teacher, and beloved community leader, reminds us that poetry moves, literally—it is active; it transcends the page's boundaries; it creates real change for real people. In her latest collection, *Backstories*, Wagner pays tribute to the transformative power of teaching, filled with its traumas, tensions, self-discoveries, and complicated victories. "Hold your hand up for silence," she writes: these poems have keen ears, and they embody listening as an action. *Backstories* is an essential collection for those who teach and those who have felt the profound influence of a compassionate teacher.

—Jenny Molberg, author of *The Court of No Record*

The poems in this latest collection of Maryfrances Wagner get much of their remarkable power from a wealth of evocative and authentic details. The poems draw one irresistibly into the the daily ebb and flow of a city high school classroom. One sees and hears the gum popping, fidgeting, dozing, glaring, and disruption. Her students' stories range in tone from comic to tragic. The "found" poem of student comments is hilarious: "Why does Poe use 'bosom'? Why doesn't he just say what it is: 'butt'?" The accounts of those suffering are heartbreaking: "To pay for his drug debt, Crystal's boyfriend offered her /for a night as payment. When she fought the dealer, / he shoved a switchblade up her vagina and twisted." Wagner's empathy for her students is clear-eyed and honest, avoiding the pitfalls of nostalgia or sentimentality. As in The Canterbury Tales, there is "all God's plenty" here among young travelers on the dicy road toward adulthood.

—William Trowbridge, author of *Father and Son*

Maryfrances Wagner's poems resonate with authenticity, some comedic, some tragic, all vibrant. In *Backstories* Wagner unveils the complexity of her students' lives, knowing as career teachers do that the key to reaching a student is in understanding as much of their story as possible. The teacher, like the poet, must see below the surface of what she is shown.

I collect student journals. Kastavas presses so hard
in his that he leaves a ghost copy on the page behind it.
In afternoon light I read it like a watermark.

Luckily, there are teachers who have proven their worth in the classroom. However, few of them are poets like Maryfrances Wagner. The poems in *Backstories* are perfectly vivid and insightful. Each word belongs where it is placed. Wagner's poems are as real as the students in the front row.

—Al Ortolani, *Controlled Burn* and the *Bull in the Ring*

Praise for *Backstories*

Maryfrances Wagner has never been a "content" provider in her life. What she has been is a teacher who truly sees her students—which explains why they were so open with her--and I'm betting that not one of the survivors whose stories, usually in their own words, she's offered here has ever forgotten her. Nor will anyone who knew the ones whose stories Ms. Wagner has had to tell for them. All that and, like nurses in ERs, she knows how to make us laugh. More power to her, I say, and to all the kids who were lucky enough to know her.

—Lola Haskins, author of *Homelight*

The beauty of these poems—and the tragedy—is their truth. The experiential, first-hand detail from lives at risk in our world. Teaching is the least appreciated of essential professions, but Wagner's dedication to her students, to witnessing, gives us fierce, empathetic, and important anthems, a poetry that saves their lives, and ours.

—Christopher Buckley, author of *Sprezzatura*

Pulling no punches, Maryfrances Wagner has written a book from the trenches of American education. It's all here, every problem, every frustration. Each poem a desk: each desk a portrait. You could weep.

—Alice Friman, author of *On the Overnight Train: New and Selected Poems*

Master poet Maryfrances Wagner turns her pen to storytelling, one of her fortes, in *Backstories*. She narrates poignant dramas of daily interactions between teacher and students. These poems pull on heartstrings as they inform, like a moment when a teacher mends a student's torn shirt. This collection is an essential resource for students, teachers, and parents.

—Denise Low, Kansas Poet Laureate (2007-09)

The Draconian Sentence   Collage   Maryfrances Wagner

ACKNOWLEDGMENTS

Thanks to the following magazines who first published these poems: *Main Street Rag, Poetry East, Vox Populi, Flint Hills Review, Bearing Witness, Laurel Review, Rattle, Prairie Winds, Wind, Concho River Review, Magnolia Review, Thorny Locust, Rockhurst Review, Portside Poetry, Salt, Voices in Italian Americana, Zingara, Kansas City Voices, Gasconade Review, Medusa's Kitchen.*

A special thanks to all the students who made me eternally grateful and to all the students who taught me as much as I taught them. You all made my life richer and fuller.

Special thanks to those who helped or supported my poems along the way: Greg Field, Gay Dust, Alice Friman, Diane Quinlan, Catherine Anderson, Robert Stewart, William Trowbridge, Alarie Tennille, Tina Hacker, Denise Low, Jason Ryberg, Lola Haskins, Jo McDougall, Christopher Buckley, Lindsey Martin-Bowen, Al Ortolani, David Anstaett, Robert C. Jones, Ann Slegman, Susan Whitmore, Silvia Kofler, Michael Simms, M. Scott Douglass, Ben Furnish, Andrea Hollander, Angela Elam, Patricia Cleary Miller, Gary Lechliter, Gary Gildner, Annie Newcomer, David Baker, Betsy Beasley, Brain Daldorph, Sue Trowbridge, Lisa Stewart, H. C. Palmer, Jenny Molberg, Janette Williams, Linda Eimer Fishell, Andrea Brookhart, Carrie Allison, Kelly Wright, Stacey Portillo, Lupe Zapien, and all the many friends and former students who have supported and encouraged me over the years.

I took years assembling this book because I worried about having the right to reveal my students' backstories that for me said so much about why they behaved as they did. Although I could tell many more, these stories are representative. I have changed names and details in these poems to protect the identity of all, but these are their stories.

The Big Pencil   Collage   Maryfrances Wagner

CONTENTS

CONTENTS

3

4

Teaching 1   Collage   Maryfrances Wagner

Teaching

In third grade, I told my family I wanted to be a teacher. For Christmas, I asked for a desk so I could start practicing. I received a miniature rolltop. The next year, I asked for a chalkboard. Then books so I could start creating lessons. By sixth grade, I had the neighbor kids over for a week of Bible school. No looking back. The passion never ebbed. I walked into my first year of high school juniors as though I'd been teaching for years. After all, I had, but what I didn't know was how much I would learn about my students, myself, human nature, and inequality during the years that I taught.

1

And in the middle of them, with filthy body, matted hair, and unwiped nose, Ralph wept for the end of innocence, the darkness of man's heart, and the fall through the air of the true, wise friend called Piggy.

Lord of the Flies —
William Golding

We lived in the flicker, the tick.

What are we? Humans? Or animals? Or savages?

The world, that understandable and lawful world, was slipping away.

The thing is - fear can't hurt you any more than a dream. Maybe there is a beast... maybe it's only us.

Too Many Thoughts About Sharpened Sticks   Collage   Maryfrances Wagner

Future?   Collage   Maryfrances Wagner

Chuck

> What are we? Humans? Animals? Savages?
> William Golding – *Lord of the Flies*

On the first day of my first class in a tiny room,
Chuck takes a seat so close he taps my desk.
Every day a Polo, dress pants, buttery loafers.

When he looks up, he flashes perfect teeth. He
stares, makes me squirm, but does his work. He's
18. I'm 21. He doesn't treat me as his teacher

ready to discuss *Lord of the Flies*. Behind his silky
voice and Gucci shoes, I see his mean. He instigates
fights and whacks small boys, particularly Juan—

thick horned-rims, buck teeth, chunky—Piggy if he
stepped from the book, and he likes order, logic.
He asks questions, ponders why Jack craves the kill.

The day after spring break, Juan asks for a restroom pass.
A minute later, Chuck dips his face close to mine and asks
to call his mother to bring his lab notes for 4th hour.

You probably wonder how I fell for that. I let him go.
I heard the story after an ambulance took Juan away.
Chuck slammed the bathroom door into Juan's face over

and over until his glasses fell off his broken nose
and cheekbone. Then he plunged Juan's head
into the toilet. By the time the gurney arrived, Juan

was unconscious. Chuck earned his last credits
on Homebound. Juan's parents moved to Texas.
A door had opened into a new darkness. Students

bumped along as that year loomed shadowy
under the care of counselors. A quiet spring
of staring into space. A time of weighing.

Rumors traveled like vapor, like stories of the beast.
We lived in the flicker, the tick. Too many stained
dreams. Too many thoughts about sharpening a stick.

Third Hour Basic English III

My first year, my principal assigned me
one class of Basic English III with no books
other than the novels the regular students read
and a workbook with only twenty lessons.
I ordered a weekly *Scholastic Magazine* with stories
and exercises, invented sentences about them
to teach punctuation. We studied their favorite
song lyrics for figures of speech. The classroom,
converted from the vice principal's former office
was long and narrow with thirty desks crammed
into three aisleless rows. Students had to move
desks to get to their desk. Not even a bookcase
could hug a wall. The closet was a converted bathroom
with two shelves, a mirror over a nonfunctioning
sink, and a missing doorknob. That first Halloween,
I brought a pumpkin full of treats and put it in my
closet. Each hour I went for the pumpkin to hand out
candy. Third hour, Donnie Watts shut the door behind
me, a door I could not open from inside. Everyone
laughed but didn't let me out. The room was ground
level. The students opened the windows and climbed
out. I could hear them laughing. I could hear my
principal on the intercom asking why my class
was playing Frisbee on the front lawn but couldn't
hear me calling from the closet. After the bell rang,
Terri climbed back inside and let me out. I filled
her purse with Snickers and Milky Ways, took
a deep breath, and smiled as the next class shuffled in.

Mending Leroy's Sweater in Composition

Leroy swaggers into my class without books
or pen, jams hands into his pockets, face
partly hidden under his black hoodie.
He stares at his desk after all questions.

Students step around him and his gym bag
to trade papers. They have always kept
their distance. His fight last weekend
after the football game gave them proof.

He waits for the principal to suspend him.
He'll be gone five school days for the fight
behind the stadium, blood scrubbed clean
now from asphalt, bats, and knuckles.

A row of stitches jags across his eyebrow.
He rocks in his seat, glares. Heads bowed,
students write comments on rough drafts.
The register hisses steam. It is snowing.

I look up. Leroy opens his hoodie to show me
the rip in his sweater, sets a button on my desk.
We stare at each other. I rummage for a needle,
point to the window where light is best.

The ground outside is covered and unmarred by tracks.
I pin the rip along the seam near his waist, think
of how to situate myself, the angle so low. He
rests a hand on my arm. I kneel beside him and sew.

Final Impressions

Every morning, I drive past the bent railing
under the willow, the spray paint still vivid,
though the crosses and wreaths are gone.

Once my students tied laminated poems
on those branches, in memory of Kathy,
one of four students I've lost this way.

The neighbors left them up all winter,
fluttering on yarn bows, some mornings
winking like Morse code.

I remember so well the day before,
Kathy reading her poem about Jeff,
her yellow bow bobbing as she shifted

from foot to foot. She sketched for us
the blue dress she'd sewn for prom
and dotted in her grandmother's pearls.

Usually she hunched quietly at her desk.
She pulled layers of hair to hide her face
and bowed her head when I asked for readers.

She pressed so hard when she wrote,
I could feel the braille of her paper,
read impressions left on the under page.

We wrote elegies to her, our eyes drifting
to jags of light reflected from her chair,
before we walked to the funeral together.

We saw her framed picture on the coffin.
She wore the blue dress, the pearls.
Perhaps it is better to go in a heat,

after the last dance beneath the mirrored
ball, breath warm on a bare shoulder,
hands moist, a rose corsage wafting

its notes; knowing at last the sweetest juices.
The moment when we press so hard
before the oncoming car spins across the lane.

Mrs. Wagner Fields Questions While Teaching Edgar Alan Poe: A Found Poem

Why aren't these stories spooky like the movies?
We have to read this whole story? Can't you just sum it up?
I heard Poe was a drug addict. Did you ever do drugs?
I don't understand how that Red Death got in there?
Why does Poe use "bosom"? Why doesn't he just say what it is: "butt?"
Does "aversion" mean one of several kinds or someone who hasn't had sex?
Why does he use so much description; can't he just tell the story?
How will I use this in real life?
The movies don't use these big words; what's a "casement"?
What if my parents don't want me to read this story?
Are there Cliff Notes for Poe or an alternative assignment?
Why would anyone name a kid Ligeia?
Have you ever used the word "termagant" or "sullied" in real life?
Can we use our notes and a dictionary on the final?
Can I just tell you what I know instead of answering the questions?
Isn't marrying your cousin illegal?
Did Poe get to see any of his stories made into movies?
Is it hard to be a famous writer like Poe?
So this guy went to all of that trouble to kill a cat?
I thought only parrots could say words like "Nevermore."

Jimmy Crates

First day with students, I assign seats
to remember 163 names. Jimmy Crates stares
out the window from a back chair and rocks
against the wall. His assigned seat is third

on the front row. *Not moving*, he says. *No choice*,
I say. He stands, lifts his chair, and tosses it,
smacking four occupied seats around him. *Not
moving*, he shouts and flicks the boy in front of him

on the cheek. *I'll sit next to geek guy with a hundred
pimples and kick his chair when I want—and behind
Rachel of long, blond hair I can braid and twist like
this.* Larry volunteers to move to Jimmy's assigned seat.

Ah, what a sweet wuss, Jimmy says. *How does this
feel, boy?* and whacks Larry on the head. I call the office
for a principal. Four boys in football jerseys rise. Jimmy
scuffles and pounds the back wall. The principal arrives,

calls for more help. Jimmy's gone for five days. He lasts
three more after he returns as agitated and jumpy
as stuttering grease. *No homework*, he announces
when I give an assignment, and *no other homework either*.

We continue with pronouns and subject-verb agreement.
He bounces up, spits on the floor, and sprints out the door.
I slam it behind him, inform the office. The security guard
nabs Jimmy in the hall. Wind rumbles the windows.

My Student Rhonda's Gift

Rhonda of tiny hands
molds a hunk of clay.

Smooths it like dough,
traces and presses in

the image of her tiny
fingers. She cuts away

excess until four fingers
and a thumb emerge

identical to her own.
In a week, glazed

and baked, it's a trivet,
a paperweight, art

she sets on my desk.
Year after year it holds

down quizzes, decorates
the chalk tray, goes

with me when I pack
the retirement box.

I will always have
Ronda's fingers,

tiny as her bones
I hugged goodbye.

My Student Jason Stares Off

When he returns to composition class,
after two weeks of absence, he stares
into space or keeps his head on his desk.
He abandons bright hockey shirts for black tees
and asks me to move him by the window.

He opens his notebook but doesn't write
and doesn't raise his hand. One morning,
he lifts both feet under his desk, shakes them
like cans of paint, and rubs his soles
on the vinyl like polishers building shine.

By winter, he wears black lipstick,
Marilyn Manson shirts and skirts,
dyes his hair, then shaves it off.
Blue circles hang under his black-lined eyes.
He pierces and studs both brows.

He clicks lip and tongue rings on his teeth,
stares outside, watches leaves blow
and dogs track through snow. He doesn't
fake-box with Nate anymore, doesn't hacky sack
in the hall before school with Dewey and Matt.

My calls home are endless rings until his grandmother
answers to say she is adopting him. She fills in
the details about the night Daryl's restaurant closed:
Jason was home tidying pencils and tucking his essay
into his backpack when the police arrived.

Across town, the robber had barged into Daryl's
through the back door, pushed Jason's mother
on her knees, and waited for her to turn the last click
on the safe's lock before he fired into her brain.

The Results of Some Hoping

Ardith is last down the steps,
the only student lugging books in a fire drill.
Like a bird, she tilts her head at me, same way
her mother, Lydia, did twenty years ago.
Red-headed Lydia sputtered and wheezed
whenever she raised a hand, all of us shifting,
setting down pens, some hoping
she'd raise those eyes above clusters of tissues,
afloat on her desk like wilted gardenias.
I untangled her from hooks and latches,
but wished just once she'd open her locker
on the first try, not call out for me to wait.
Lydia, the only girl unable to run a lap,
dribble a ball, the single pep squad member
waving a crew-sweatered arm
among cheering v-necks, the lone girl
stumbling down bus aisles,
snagging her spiral on jackets.
At the door, Ardith leans
into her sliding geometry book.
A pencil and highlighter bounce off her elbow.
We shoo her into open air, scramble for books
fluttering pages behind her.
As she measures the last step with a toe,
her red hair spirals in the wind;
a flurry of Kleenex lifts from her purse like doves.

Kastavas Puts It On the Line

In my writing class, Brian nudges Kastavas awake,
Sleep at night, Dude. Kastavas jolts up from
a pool of drool. *Fuck you, skater! Dude! I work late.*
The students snap face left, stare at Kastavas—then me.

I lean on one foot, then the other, chew my cheek,
tap a pencil, dip into the drawer for a Write Up form.
Yesterday Kastavas handed me two sonnets and an essay.
I know how he lives. I know about his father.

He smears an inked heart on his desk.
You know the rules, I say and slap a Write Up
in front of him. *I'll see you after class.*
He slumps across the room to sharpen a pencil.

I collect student journals. Kastavas presses so hard
in his that he leaves a ghost copy on the page behind it.
In afternoon light I read it like a watermark.

How Ryan Strong Became The Most Talked About Boy

He set no football or track records. No
oboe awards at State, and he didn't score
highest on his ACT or earn a Bright Flight.

He wasn't the prankster in biology
or the hacky sack star in hallways, wasn't
invited to pool parties or gaming nights,

but he invited Janette, as quiet and unnoticed
as a shelved book, to homecoming. A crisp
October night, the final football score a win.

For courage, Ryan swigged from a pint
his brother gave him. Janette said she wanted
to be a nurse. He said he hadn't decided.

Under the spinning mirror ball, he watched
light glister across her face as they swayed.
Her perfume encircled them. He pulled her closer.

On the way home, he wanted to see how fast
his Mustang could go, but the wheel bucked.
Swerved. The car smashed into the side rail,

then into the oak he passed every morning.
Janette flew through the windshield and never
woke up. They were sixteen. Ryan missed the rest

of the year. He didn't think when he left that night
with an orchid in a box and a suit jacket over his arm
that he'd become the most talked-about boy in school.

Third Hour Grammar Exercises in May

Each checked another's paper,
and somewhere around sentence
ten, I was lying on a beach towel.

Only a small part of my brain stayed
to name the subordinate clause in each
sentence. I worried the students would

discover me gone. I scanned the room,
saw some poised with red pen awaiting
the next answer. Others, like me, weren't

there either. Their glassy eyes gazed
into space, their minds, perhaps, a few
yards away, at the same Hawaiian beach.

Ten minutes later, in the hall, I keep
runners to a power walk, shaking my head
at roaming hands of sweethearts. Mr. Bailey

nods as two sophomores show him
their new retainers, one a Batman cape,
the other a watermelon. Ms. Dust grades.

I lean against a locker, arms crossed,
as we teachers pass the familiar eye lock
down the hall. One slaps the wall, another

stands in prayerful repose. It's early spring,
nearly prom. Sun filters through overcast
and lays a strip of light at our feet.

Remembering Eric Sanders

We didn't take him seriously
the day he cruised through the parade
in a convertible, his shaved head
sunburned around his crossbones tats.
The safety pin in his ear glinted.
We thought he was getting in character
for a play. Behind a bullhorn, the boy
always open for a chat, who loved chess
and drama, said we needed to build
a shelter, stock up on water and jerky.
Said Neo-Nazis had formed camps to blow
us up, send us in pieces across a crowded
sky. He said killing is a mysterious passion
and every citizen has a prepared place
under a burial blanket. We shrugged
from our places within the parade crowd,
but raised our melting blue snow cones.
The next Monday during lunch, he
streaked across the school parking lot
after he tossed a cherry bomb in a toilet.
To calm his new rage, we tried a fist bump,
but he turned away and huffed.
Once the angel in the fifth-grade play,
the one to suffer wasp stings to bring
cornflowers to Ellie, alone in the hospital
with mono. When he drove off a cliff
into that good night, we talked about it
for weeks, counselors scheduled process
sessions, and we kept wondering. Bill printed
Eric's motto "Individuality highlights our
difference; respect brings us together"
from when he ran for class president. We
pitched in to get it engraved on a plaque
we hoped the principal might hang in the hall.

Cut and Inked

> "Of course they hurt, but in a good way."
> —Sparrow Meade

Like the sound of bees,
needles open blossoms
of oozing blood.

The artist stipples
tracings, pounds ink
into red and black

blurs, invades that
secret hideout where grief
sleeps in skin's cellar.

With each carved line,
the dark melds with pain's
elixir—a temporary fix.

Too quickly
the cuts close,
crust, and heal.

Disappearing

The first year, Crystal argued about too many exercises,
too many papers, and her attitude outgunned us all.

In a dream I had, someone handed me a baby
wrapped in a soiled blanket. I took it outside to see the stars.

In October, Crystal, pregnant, dropped out of school.
The counselors said nothing. Homecoming distracted us.

When I realized I left the baby outside, I ran back out.
The baby didn't cry. Its lips were blue. It slept deeply.

The next year, Crystal was back in my class. She didn't speak
except when asked a question. She stared into her hands.

She stared into space. Her eyes were buried coins. She came
to my desk to ask what to write about. *Tell your story*, I said.

I brought the baby back inside to feed it, but its mouth was gone.
A skinny stray roamed the yard. Sniffed where the baby had lain.

To pay off his drug debt, Crystal's boyfriend offered her
for a night as payment. When she fought the dealer,

he shoved a switchblade up her vagina and twisted.
The boyfriend beat her before taking her to the hospital.

I gave the dog a dish of kibble. I rocked the baby in my arms.
Its eyes stayed closed. Parts of it started disappearing.

Tonight on the news, a pregnant woman couldn't drive fast enough
to the hospital. She swerved through a rail and flew into a ditch.

In those airborne moments, she delivered the baby. The police
found the mother's neck broken. The baby rolled under the seat.

Still breathing. One policeman wrapped the cold baby in a soiled blanket and ran to the ambulance through a night frosty with stars.

Crystal didn't bleed to death. Surgery helped. No more sex. No babies. The boys were out on parole. Crystal turned sixteen and told her story.

Ends

> Lord, let us feel pity. . .and sorrow for ourselves
> and all the angel warriors that fall.
> —Walter Dean Myers, *Fallen Angels*

What about the end? the teacher asks his seniors.
How has Perry changed in Fallen Angels?

They shrug and look around. One wears
an ankle monitor for robbing Pizza Hut

with his cousin. Several say their fathers
served. Like Perry, they came back different.

Most miss at least one day a week. Most
often suspended or asleep at their desks.

Fourth hour is lunch. On their shift, the boys
talk about fighting, but not war. They talk about

their first time doing time and what to expect—
three meals, cable, heating and air—far better

than darkness after late shifts at McDonald's.
They talk about sponsors. Each day, the teacher

crosses off a date on his white board calendar.
He twists his ear gauges, these rose gold plugs

bigger than last week's crossbones. He stares
out the window at a broad shadow on the lawn.

What would you have done if trapped?
He describes weekends of body suspension,

how it doesn't hurt as much as they'd
think. They nod. He has fifteen piercings.

His arm tats tell a Chinese honor story. On his neck
a red wheelbarrow and white chickens.

Cafeteria Lady

Her hairnet, a spiderweb
above her eyebrows,
her white uniform
speckled with cinnamon,
her buttons stretched tight
in torn holes,
not once does she
speak or smile as
we scoot our trays
down silver rails,
and she scoops stewed fruit
or runny cobbler,
gazes past us
through a window
opened to a world
we cannot see.

2

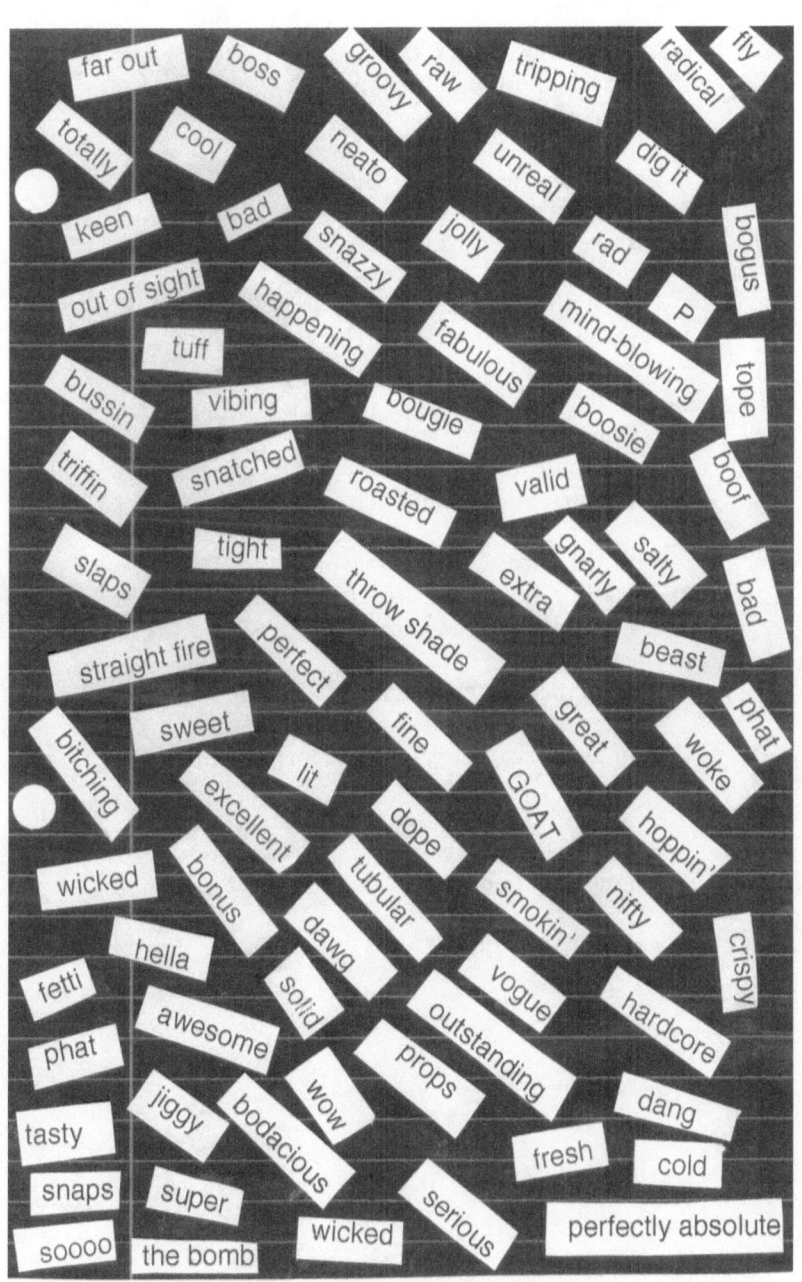

Teaching 2   Collage   Maryfrances Wagner

The Sophomores

Crunch ice, suck candies,
smack, blow bubbles, stretch
gum to arm's length. They

shift, wiggle, squiggle drawings
of trolls and vampires. They
sigh, roll their eyes, giggle.

They snicker, whisper, turn around,
crack knuckles, stab notebooks,
conk their heads into their hands.

They frown, they scowl, they look down,
stare out windows, into space, into
mirrors, fiddle in their book bags

to send texts or answers while
staring ahead. They ask questions
already answered, pick debris

from their braces, click binders
like teeth , rattle keys, stuff wrappers
under desks, spray cologne, forget pens,

ask why. Under desks their shoes scuffle,
shuffle like puppies pulling on leashes,
long, lazy hounds blocking the aisles.

The Sophomores Study Julius Caesar:
A Found Poem

Why would a senator wear a toga
or an athlete run in a skirt?

Will tapping a woman with a thong
really make her pregnant?

Does Julius Caesar want fat men
around him so he'll look buff?

Does it mean that Cassius is starving
if he has a lean and hungry look?

Was he a Publicist, no, I mean a Presbyterian
who ran through the streets shouting?

Why didn't he just say, *They're going to kill you?*
No one knows what *Beware the Ides of March* means.

Isn't Greece in Rome?
I think it is.

I don't get this B.C. thing. How did they know He was
coming? Were they just hoping he'd come on the right day?

If it's a deer, why does Shakespeare call it a hart,
and how do signs get inside the body of animals for people to read?

Wow, that Portia stabbed herself and swallowed fire.
I wish my girlfriend would stab herself in the leg for me.

Look at this library book full of statues of Julius Caesar
and Mark Antony. They must have read Shakespeare.

By the end of this play, we're all
going to want to run on our swords.

None of this makes sense to me, but I know a test is coming.
Are you saying Julius Caesar was a real person?

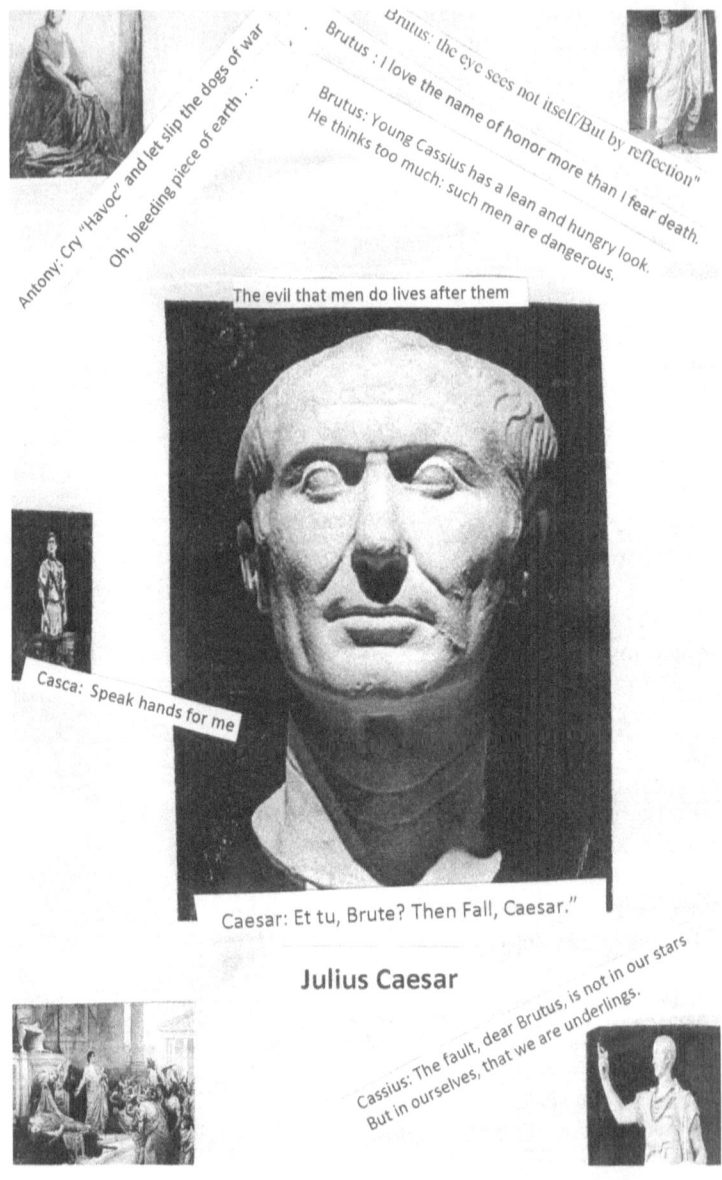

Brutus: the eye sees not itself/But by reflection"

Brutus : I love the name of honor more than I fear death.

Brutus: Young Cassius has a lean and hungry look.
He thinks too much: such men are dangerous.

Antony: Cry "Havoc" and let slip the dogs of war

Oh, bleeding piece of earth . . .

The evil that men do lives after them

Casca: Speak hands for me

Caesar: Et tu, Brute? Then Fall, Caesar."

Julius Caesar

Cassius: The fault, dear Brutus, is not in our stars
But in ourselves, that we are underlings.

That Fault in Ourselves   Collage   Maryfrances Wagner

My Sophomores View the Eclipse

While reading Julius Caesar,
we set aside Brutus's soliloquy
to poke pinholes into paper,
tear a second sheet for viewing.
Today, we have permission to view the eclipse.
Mickey, without permission, explains,
again, the process they've already heard.
Worthy of her role as Casca,
Emily stabs her paper five times
then checks the mirror in her purse
where the eye sees not itself/ But by reflection.
At 11:30 they spill down the steps,
like runners on Lupercal, and scatter
out the door, warning each other not to look up.
They line up their sheets of paper,
see half a moon, half a sun.
Ramone, who loves honor more,
lifts his face and hands to the sky.
See, nothing happens, he insists, impervious
yet to wrinkles or words blurry on a page.
These are the years of unquenched
weekend thirst, when t-shirts sport
skulls and crossbones or announce No Fear.
I watch my students view the sun secondhand,
with only a pinhole of light.
When we shuffle back to Brutus,
they wait for me, who thinks too much,
to explain what the lines really mean.

The Sophomores Study Grammar:
A Found Poem

Why do we have to study grammar? We already know
how to speak and understand each other.

You expect us to learn all of this in one unit?
I've never heard of a verbal in my life, only gerbils.

Are you saying particles or pedophiles?
What if nobody ever taught us grammar before?

If nobody says it like that, why do we
have to learn the right way to say it?

Can't you just overlook the little errors? If my mother
can't figure out these clauses, how do you expect me to?

You want us to do all of these in one night?
What if my parents won't let me stay up that late?

You expect us to know how to use a semicolon?
We barely know what one Is!

A thing I know about agreement is
you come to a conclusion on differences.

How can this be a derogatory sentence?
I thought words were derogatory.

I asked three people last night if they knew
the comma rules, and not one of them did.

We never stop learning in here do we?
Is it too late to drop this class?

Fledgling

Trimming back the straggling spirea, I thought
of Melissa in sophomore English telling the class
she never had a curfew. She wrote in her journal
about her cousin Terry rubbing against her, skin
to skin, in the dark. Now, barely fifteen, she had
Aaron to raise. She said she watched Terry shoot
Brian in the eye. It was no accident, she said,
and he wasn't sorry either. He lied to get off.

Clipping twigs into bundles, I startled two
baby blue jays, more stomach than wing,
bumping around in the marigolds. They hopped
into the garage and smacked beaks on the floor.
When I pipered them back out near their mother's
caw, they collided into each other and squawked.
I shooed Whiskers, the neighbor's cat, back
to his own yard and left the jays to stumble

through their flying lesson. By afternoon they'd
skimmed the lawn but never quite lifted. I hung
my clippers, still thinking of Melissa dropping out
to stay with the baby after she brought him home
from daycare bruised and scalded. By morning,
when I reached for the paper in the driveway, two
flattened tufts were smears in the street, a single
tail feather, barely formed, stirred in the wind.

How can I still have an "F" if I turned everything in?

A found poem from sophomore English classes

If Nicole had a baby in Japan,
would her baby be Japanese?
Will it start speaking in Japanese?

Aren't windmills to cool the earth
and prevent global warming? Aren't
they like those pumping oil wells?

What do you mean about not keeping
marine animals in captivity? What does
captivity mean? Can animals join the marines?

Is it true that if you cut off the body
of a salamander it will grow another one?
I know worms can.

What does it mean to take something
for granite. Does that mean you hold
it like a rock or pretend it's granite?

Do we live in North America? Who
decided that? What about the Canadians?
And how can Chicago be in Illinois if it's a state?

Is Alice Walker's book *The Color Purple*
about Prince? Do you think she knew him?
Do you think Michael Jackson was a pedophile?

My dad quit pop. Now he drinks beer instead.
He found out pop kills you. Would you quit
drinking pop if you knew it killed you? Not me.

After Columbine and the End of Believing It Was the Last Time

Among those seeking counselors
or cowering in hallways, aspirants

hunkered, kept quiet. When *Time*
published Columbine cover stories

two weeks in a row, we talked about it
in class. I passed both issues around, but

by the end of the period, only one
returned. I asked for whoever had it

to turn it in please, but no one did.
I suspected who tucked it in a notebook.

It wasn't the boy cutting his arms at night
then opening the wounds in class

with a pen. It wasn't the boy flicking
and clicking his tongue stud over and over

against his teeth. It wasn't the girl whose
mother didn't report her boyfriend's

molestation of her six-year-old sister. No
one returned the magazine, and no one

ratted. That night, a friend called to talk
about the shooting. Couldn't get it out

of her head. Kept looking at the stop sign outside
where a boy hunched under a trench coat,

smoking. She said she could see into the window
next door where someone else was staring out

at the boy smoking. *I'm going to dream about this
tonight*, she said. *It's going to be Klebold.*

It seemed clear that wars were not made by generations and their special stupidities, but that wars were made instead by something ignorant in the human heart.

Blue paint is the river flowing away from Devon.

A Separate Peace

THE CLASSIC AMERICAN NOVEL

I began to know that each morning reasserted the problems of night before, that sleep suspended all but changed nothing, that you couldn't make yourself over between dawn and dusk.

. . . recreate what we need: Finny still in the tree . . .

Up a Tree   Collage   Maryfrances Wagner

Dioramas

> Everyone has a moment in history which
> belongs particularly to him.
> —John Knowles, *A Separate Peace*

The sophomores hand in dioramas,
thirty quiet settings on the counter,

chosen moments of late-night projects
lined up like caves or eggs, waiting

for someone to wander in, recreate
what we need: Finny still in the tree,

Jack still a choirboy on an off-scale
island. Shoebox moments suspended

like young faces in photos
where everyone is laughing.

Blue paint is the river flowing away
from Devon, tide pools on the island.

Characters stand suspended
as long as paper mâché and paint hold.

Perfect imperfection,
lives held still in our hands.

Chapter By Chapter

> Reading is a psycholinguistic guessing game.
> —Kenneth Goodman
> Reading is a very complex process that requires a great deal
> of active participation [from] the reader. —Jianfei Chen

A faceted glass cat in April sunlight
casts a hundred options.
Inside cake mixes, hidden recipes.
Under labels, remedies.
Inside out, tight, machined
seams hide loose threads.
A dozen ribboned letters behind
socks unravel secrets in a drawer.
Chapter by chapter, mica stripped
of its glitter, one page at a time.
A dozen trapped backstories
fly from an attic trunk
like moths
finished with wool.

Teaching 3   Collage   Maryfrances Wagner

Hope   Collage   Maryfrances Wagner

3

The Detention Suite

During my years of teaching, rather than have students receive in-school suspension for classroom infractions, I held my own detention after school where students would spend thirty minutes doing homework in my classroom. Often only one student was in a detention and would start telling me his/her/ their story. I learned much more about students I never would have discovered otherwise. There is always a backstory.

Brandon Langford Talks Through Detention

I'm here because I don't want a suspension,
but I hope you know you caused me to miss my bus.
I don't even understand why I have detention.
You tell us to say what we think. I spoke
my thoughts, and that's my right. My dad
does it all the time, freedom of speech,
and we cheer. Well, we did. He's a combat vet,
but now he's in prison for child porn
and hitting my mom. She's glad he's gone.
Do I have to stay here the whole time?
If I'm nice, can I leave early? You could even
drive me home if you want. My house is four
miles from here. My mom works. You wouldn't
want me to sit outside until ten would you?
I don't know what to write my narrative on.
Maybe you could give me some ideas. Do you
like fish? I have tropical fish. I could write about that.
Have you ever been to a fish show? Bet you
didn't even know there was such a thing.
I won first place in the last show. I set up
a great tank, and all of my fish have babies.
I like guppies best. I once had a mother
die in childbirth, but the baby lived. I still have him.
My fantails are beauties, and I have gouramis
and cichlids. My mom says they calm me down.
You probably want me to shut up and do homework,
write that narrative for your class. I already did my math.
I'm good at math. I'm not good at raising my hand
before I talk. This I know. I can do my timetables
up to fives. My math teacher taught me how to do them
on my knuckles. Do you want me to show you?
Nah, you probably want to grade papers
and ignore me. I get it. My mom does that too.
She turns the tv louder. You wouldn't mind
taking me home would you? You could see my fish.

Danielle Dances in a Mosh Pit

What did you do
last weekend?

You probably
sharpened pencils

or bought
new red pens.

I'm only
kidding.

Me and Carly went
to a headbanger

and danced
in a mosh pit.

We were the only
girls in there.

The guys
wore chains

and had
tons of ink.

Carly dislocated
her shoulder,

and someone
with steel boots

kicked me
in the eye.

It was
so cool.

Niki Comes in Complaining

I still don't know why I'm here. I'm one of your best
students. I turn in my work, and I read the dreadful
literature you assign us like it means something
to me. I probably should zip my mouth before I say
what I think, but how can I relate to Hester Pryne?
I want to read one book where teachers don't
have to prepare us with, *These were the attitudes
of the time.* Please. I want to read a book
with a good role model where a black man
doesn't have to fight the system, and I don't mean
a black author because that's what they write
about too. It's all negative. How do black writers
think that's going to make me feel good? I want
to read something where a black man is successful
or a black woman doesn't have to do more than
everyone else before someone notices. I want to be
a successful black woman someday, and I'm not
going to get there by reading classics. Maybe
that's why I like math and science. I'm going to be
an engineer, not a reader of classics. Speaking
of classics, do we have to see *Christmas Carol*
again this year? I've been dragged there every year
since sixth grade, and I can recite some of the lines,
especially where Belle leaves because Scrooge likes
money more. Nothing wrong with liking both
money and love. I know I'll make a lot more money
as an engineer than as a teacher. Maybe someday
someone will tell my story about Niki, the successful
engineer, and all of her children went to college.

Brandy Ambles into Detention to Tell Me Her Story

I missed my bus to come here. I hope
my boyfriend will pick me up, or I'll have
a long walk. This is the only place I can
do homework. You have no idea what life's
like at my house. We live in a motel room.
It's a big room, but I have six brothers and one
sister. My mom and dad are rarely there, so I
babysit. My brothers are demons. Better hope
you don't get them. The baby has fallen off the bed
three times, and the last time had to go to hospital,
and it's ALWAYS noisy. We go outside during
summer because the air conditioner doesn't work,
but in winter, Mom won't let us outside in the dark,
and that means I can't walk to a library to type my essay.
You'll have to take it handwritten 'cuz I can't get here
before school either. We're going to an apartment
when my daddy gets some overtime. He had a good job
as a mechanic. We lived in a house with a fenced-in yard
but he got laid off. Now he's at Walmart until he can find
another mechanic job. At least it's quiet in here, but I
don't see how I can ever read a whole novel unless
I read it right here. My history teacher said if we don't
know history, we're doomed to repeat it. Yeah, I failed
history and have to take it again. I'll probably be here a lot.

Brianna Shows Up to Detention

I know I don't have detention, but can I
sit here and do my homework? I know
you're disappointed in my grades, but my
life has really changed. My mom took a job
in Nebraska, and she never sees my dad
anyway since he's a truck driver. Now he goes
where she is in Nebraska. My brother left
months ago. I don't mind being alone. My
boyfriend knows how to cook. He's why
my mom didn't take me to Nebraska. He's
black, and she told me to break up with him
or she was done with me. My dad sold our
house and said he wasn't home enough to keep
paying bills. I stay in my car or at my boyfriend's,
only his mother feels like mine. She wants him
to break up with me because I'm white, and I'm
pregnant. She said she'd take care of me if I'll give
her the baby. My boss fired me since I was showing
and running to the bathroom so much. Now, I can't
afford gas, but I get a free breakfast and lunch here,
so that helps. I stay with friends when they offer, so
I get showers and my clothes washed. It's getting
colder, so I'll probably live at my boyfriend's and try
to decide what to do after I have to give up the baby.
I know I've been in your classes for two years, and you've
seen a better me, but what would you do in my situation?

Melissa Powers Talks Through Detention

Are you kidding me? I can't sleep during this stupid
detention? I have to go to work at 5:00. You hear
what I'm saying, and I don't get off till ten, so I
could use a nap, but I have something to work on.
I hope it can be for another class, or do I have to slog
through that Poe story with words I can't pronounce?
I mean really, who ever says *casement* or *termagant*?
Why not say *window* and *bitch*. Then we wouldn't
have to read a dictionary to understand his stories.
And why does he put all that description in there?
Can't he just tell the story? You know, it'd help
if you'd let us write papers in teams. Think of
the time we'd save. You'd have fewer papers to grade.
You can thank me for that great idea. How hard is it
to become a famous writer like Poe or Twain? Twain
didn't use correct grammar in his stories. He didn't set
a good example for budding writers. Honestly, I don't
want to read these stories. I only want to read my own
writing, and I like the way I write it the first time.
I don't need to do all of that revision you think it needs.
And I don't know why I can't use abstract words
when the whole point is that I want to be abstract.
It makes me more mysterious. It makes people want
to ask me questions. Some things I'll never understand.

Scott Whittington III Stoops to Detention

I should not have to be here.
Do you know who my father is?
He has a street named after him.
He could get you into so much trouble.
At the least, you can expect a call.
Right now, he's in New York, closing
a business deal for more money
than you'd see in a lifetime of teaching.
You've probably never been to New York.
It's too expensive for teachers. If I have
to sit in here, I'm going to talk. All you said
was I had to serve thirty minutes. I'm
watching the time here on my new Rolex.
I'm staying with my cousin this week
while my mother has new carpeting put in.
She's also going to a spa for a couple of days.
I wish I had a brother sometimes so we could
game together instead of playing with virtuals.
Even the chess games I play aren't with real
people. My mom didn't want any more kids.
She and my dad like their spare time to be their
own. I'll probably feel that way too when I'm
older and settled into my own business life. I stay
with my grandmother a lot. She bakes brownies.
My mother doesn't cook, of course. She is a neat
freak and doesn't like dirtying up the kitchen.
She doesn't like anyone roughhousing or getting
too close to her Herend figurines. Some of hers
could be in museums. I'm hoping my cousin and I
can go see the new Spiderman movie or maybe
go to Worlds of Fun. I've never been there. I hear
you can ride the Zambezi Zinger and see shows.
My parents prefer opera and symphonies.
It's almost been thirty minutes. Can I go now?

Lidia Overshares

We study the Bible at home. My mom reads
her favorite parts to us and says God loves us
all of the time, but why does he tell Abraham
to kill his son or bless the sons who killed their
brother, or flood the world, or make it so people
can't talk to each other? Look what David got away
with. Don't get me started on questions I ask. My
mother says God wasn't really going to let Abraham
kill his son. He was only testing his faith, and my
youth minister says God works in mysterious ways
and the New Testament isn't like that, but God
killed his own son, so how is that different? I
asked him who could do any of that today and get
away with it? Murder, rape, and mayhem, I said,
but he turned out the light and touched me
where only your husband is supposed to touch. I
guess he thought if God loves us all of the time,
it must be okay for him, a messenger of God. He
kept doing that on Wednesdays, always saying
he needed to see me after class, and I didn't
tell my mom because he was my minister,
and I was afraid. I wanted to write my narrative
about it, but I figured one or both of us might
get into trouble. I stopped going to church instead.
My mother asks why, but I'm afraid to tell her.
And that's not all. The minister's son is a student here,
and he does the same thing. Like father like son.
Like David. Like Amnon. Like Shechem. If we
are all born sinners because Adam and Eve
ate some fruit, that's a long grudge if you ask me.
I read parts my mother doesn't share. If I
write about this, do you have to tell anyone?

Terrill Wakes Up from Nodding Off

Sorry, I know we're not supposed to sleep
in detention. I was up late at the hospital
because of my dad. That's why I didn't get
my homework done. I wanted to stay, but
my mom said I'd be better off going to school
and trying to have a normal day. I don't know
how she thinks that's possible. I have six little
sisters and a brother. They'd be a handful if
something bad happens to my dad. My mom
has a good job, but that's a lot of kids to raise
alone. He'd expect me to be the man of the family,
but I know he wants me to go to college. I've got
a full ride as a scholar athlete, but I don't know
about going away if my mom's left alone. I know
it looked like I ignored you when you asked if you
could put my paper on the board. I don't know.
I don't really want people to know I'm a good
student. I want them to remember me as a star
athlete. That's really what I do best anyway.
I don't mind writing, but I'm not sure I want
anyone else to know what I said in that essay
or to know I wrote well enough to be on display.
See what I'm saying? I'm not thinking clearly
because my dad was shot again. That's why he's
in the hospital. He said he didn't think he was
going to make it this time. He wasn't doing
anything wrong, just sitting at a diner eating
a tuna sandwich beside the wrong person.

Holly Keeps on Talking Through Detention

Well, here I am, and I'm gonna try not to talk
nonstop since that's the reason I'm here, but
you know me. Mostly, I can't help myself like
when Jeff Ball was nominated for homecoming
queen. That was big news. The principal's trying
to squash the nomination, but the ACLU said
Jeff had his rights like the time Darrell wore
that Satan Rules t-shirt, and the ACLU said
he had the right to any religion, but if Jeff
gets the most votes for homecoming queen,
it will start a *poo pah*. See, I remember that from
Cat's Cradle. Shows you I listen. Because I talk
doesn't mean I'm not a good student. Anyway,
the principal ought to clean out his own house.
Students talk about him driving Erica around
after school, and he ignores that his vice principal
is *making the beast with two backs* with the head
cheerleader. I remember that from *Othello* even
though I didn't like that play or Othello. We all
were saying that line. My mother said when she
was a student, nothing much ever happened.
The biggest news was someone pulling the fire
alarm, a sudden fight in the hall, or the day everyone
went outside for the solar eclipse and the school
president streaked nude across the parking lot.
My mother says even a perfect child can burn down
a house whatever that's supposed to mean.

Levon the Repeat Offender

Boy, I'm sure in detention a lot. Why don't you
just send me to the principal and let me get
suspended. I could have three days shooting hoops
and hanging out with my friends. Good times.
These detentions must get old for you having
to hang out after school with us. I know you
wanna turn me into a good student like Terry
or Tonya. You keep telling me about my potential.
Well, what you don't know is I've got a rep. I can't
mess up how my friends see me. See what I'm
saying? Nah, you wouldn't understand. Nothing
personal about you. Well, maybe a little because you
demand more than most of us think you should. I'm
not alone in this thinking. All this writing and reading
takes time I don't have. After school, I play
basketball. I'm training. I'm good. I like those
cooperative teams you set up, though.
People explain things to me that I don't get.
I can't be raising my hand to ask questions, but my
team explains how to do things. You do that too
with us sometimes, but then everyone knows
we're getting help. It's about the cred. It's not
like Saudi who acts out because he can't read
and doesn't want anyone to know. People
expect me to act up. Teachers get used to it. Not
you. No offense, but one thing, though, is in here
I get homework done. I'm signing up for your
second semester class. Ha. Surprise. If I'm
in your class, I'll serve some detention, but you're
going to make sure I pass. Put us in teams. What's a
few hours after school if everyone thinks I'm doing
my homework because I have to in detention.

Libby Steps in for Her Brother Connor

Hey, I know I'm not the one who's
supposed to serve detention, but I'm
Connor's proxy today. He has to work
a baseball game. He's one of the lucky
ones who got a job with the Royals.
He's also been busy looking up sources
on hemp for his research paper. Your
class is one of the few he attends. He wants
that college credit even though he's late.
After all, it's first hour. He has a ton
of excuses for missing other classes.
My mom would have called about this
detention because we don't ever get
into trouble, but she's out of town this
month with my dad. She goes to help
with his business, plus see the world
and buy cool clothes no one else will be
wearing. Connor and I can handle ourselves.
Our parents think we're responsible, and we
are. We're good students aren't we-- even if
we don't eat home-cooked meals or sleep
enough. Connor really stays up too late,
and I tell him to go to bed. That's why
he falls asleep in class. Our life is nothing
like my friend Jenna's. Her mom doesn't work
and greets her with snacks when she gets home.
Sometimes, we have dinner there. Our parents
decided we didn't need a nanny anymore. We
even pay bills if they're gone a long time. Our
neighbor wanted to report our family, but she
didn't. Don't worry. We'll get through life
sturdier than most, maybe a little late and untidy,
but we'll be there. I'm even thinking
about becoming a teacher. Do what you do.

Brian Baker Dishes Out

Do you wonder at all why I hide in the hall
or want passes to the bathroom? I hate
working in groups. They hand me the questions
and say, *You're the one, man,* like that's going
to make me wanna help them. Anything I say
hangs in the air like a comic bubble. I'm
in the wrong place. I like to read Aristotle,
and everyone looks at me like I'm trying
to suck up. Who would I be sucking up to?
You've never assigned Aristotle. I read
Homer and Shakespeare too, and I don't
need your help. You should leave me alone
and be happy that I am busy learning.
After school I work for my Dad, scooping
ice cream for kids who don't know
who Aristotle is, and neither does
my father, but their fathers don't own
a Baskin-Robbins like mine, so they aren't
scooping ice cream every night instead
of reading like I want to do. What they've
learned to do is work the system and say
how hard they have it. I know you think
I'm disrespectful, but who's rewarding those
of us asking questions? Wondering about things?
Ignoring those making fun of us for doing
our homework. Isn't it someone like me who
might make a difference? I could become
an innovator or a scientist even though I really
want to be a writer. I wanted to ask if we could
read Sartre and talk about existentialism. Then,
I look around and hit my head and say to myself,
Forget it, Brian, and scoop ice cream after school
because no one here cares who Sartre is, but they'll
come for two dips of Rocky Road or Peach
instead of completing your homework assignment,
and even though I could be learning better things,
I'll have my assignment when I come to class.

Carlos Martinez Has His Say in Detention

Some teachers overlook little things,
like talking or nor having homework. I laugh
in the face of homework, and I'm not giving
back this pencil I borrowed because you gave me
detention. It's mine now. You expect too much,
and those emails you send my mom do no good.
She shows them to me, and we laugh. She lets me
be, and I let her be even though I've watched her
hide vodka under pillows or behind plants. All day,
she packs boxes and aches when she gets home. She
agrees that great writers don't have to know how
to spell or punctuate or write in complete sentences.
Editors handle that. Get our ideas down. Lackeys
do the rest. Use our genius for other things. Mom
uses hers to make afghans and booties. She's
learning to cook, but so far burns everything,
and she adds things that don't go together in casseroles
we throw out. She'll get it, though. My aunt bought her
a cookbook, but we don't have the stuff she needs.
We look at recipes and talk about what we'd like to eat.
Then we eat macaroni and cheese. We only have to add
milk. Sometimes we slice hot dogs and put cheese inside.
They're good. You may not realize this, but I have
a history of insubordinate behavior. It's a habit
I can't break. I don't let the school take my picture
either. I wear sunglasses so no one can see my eyes,
and, so you know, I hate vocabulary. Who cares as long
as we get across what we want to say? Cavemen didn't know
many words, and they understood each other. I got two
percent on the vocabulary part of my state test, but everyone
says I understand very well. Besides, that test is worthless.
I didn't even answer half of them. What did you get when you
took this test? I'll bet not many. Why does it bother you
that I talk like I do? I talk that way to everyone—teachers,
my mom, principals. No one cares. They ignore
everything I do, but you wouldn't know about that.

Homewok   Collage   Maryfrances Wagner

4

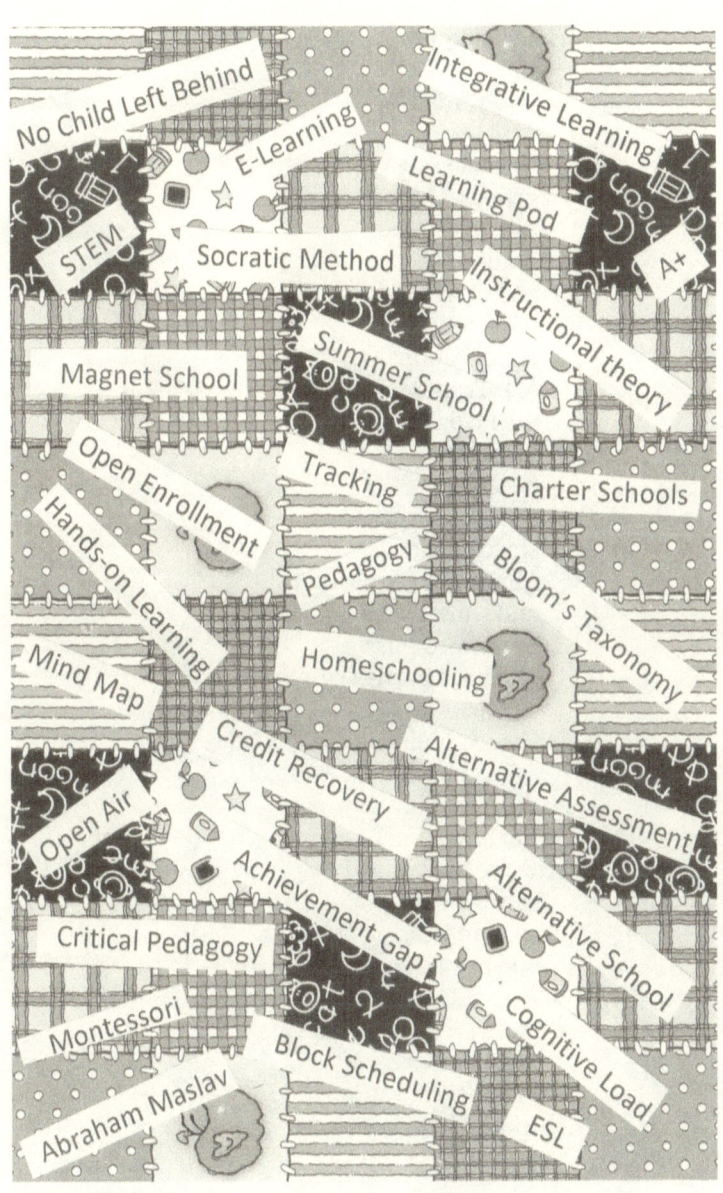

Teaching 4   Collage   Maryfrances Wagner

Cameron Brings Me Cake

Even though
I
really, really
hate you
because you
give us
too much
homework
and assign
too many
compositions,
Ms. Trundle,
my favorite
teacher
because
she lets us
sing French
Christmas Carols
and work French
crossword puzzles
and have parties
to celebrate
French holidays,
asked me to bring you
this piece of
Bûche de Noël
we've been
eating today,
so here it is,
and even though
I
really, really
wanted to
I didn't
spit on it.

Prompt

I ask my students to jot down
Anything someone might

consider a secret. **We'll get
ideas for your next story.**

Stacey tilts her head.
Brandon stares at his desk.

Here is a box, I say, **to put them in.**
Can we make them up? **Of course.**

**I expect you to make them up.
Here is my secret.**

I fold and toss it in the box.
The box becomes a folded flurry.

You can add more tomorrow.
What if we want to tell a real secret?

**Fine. Don't tell me if your secret's true.
I'd be obligated to tell.**

Can we read a few today? **Sure.**
My mother is really my sister.

*My cousin's in prison, not away at college.
I am not a citizen.*

*My dad is cheating on my mom.
My mom's boyfriend raped my sister.*

That's enough for today.

Looking Back on Giving Harvey a Lift to School

The school remodeling brought down every wall.
Out came oak closets, bookcases, cabinets.
I stood in the room that once was Harvey's
and remembered mornings driving him to school.

Tapping on his briefcase, Harvey stared in silence
at falling leaves and store fronts. I pictured him
at night in a lamp halo marking math quizzes.
Every morning, a cloud of Old Spice followed him,

and I bravoed the ties he wore—assorted thunderbolts
and blue jays and cardinals from his bird collection.
Every afternoon, when I stood in his doorway, ready
to drive us home, he was erasing math formulas.

Spitballs and footprinted homework hovered near chairs.
His sad eyes reflected in his glass-front cabinets.
Rumors followed him down hallways to the lunchroom
where he ate pickle-loaf sandwiches from brown bags.

He stayed tucked into himself like a folded table,
letting his crows or chartreuse thunderbolt ties express
his thoughts, until he raged one day, his ears red, his
eyes full of lightning, that not everyone cared

to be included, to drink wine or to dance at parties.
By spring, I didn't drive him anymore, and I saw him
only at meetings, staring off, orioles or larks in flight
on his ties. By June his suitcase banged next

to others on the bus ride back to Nebraska. Now,
so many years later, the slate boards are gone,
the staircase I once dashed down is a plastered wall.
I watch new staff members scoot past me, down

wider hallways, and I am on the verge of a
new past, the old one erasing its hard evidence,
but there in my mind is Harvey waiting for the bus,
his red thunderbolt a fire about to take off.

In Search of Le Mot Juste

I troll through the sea of words,
throwing back those bearded ones.
It's too late for *hath* and *thee,* or those
vague slippery ones: *factor* and *trait.*

I slosh past slimy mates:
soon and *moon, bait* and *late,*
let *cosmos* and *fear* wiggle off free.
They're bottom feeders I don't need.

Near the cliffs, *was taken* and *to be*
lie stagnant in pools, worth
no more than those tattlers
exciting or *sad* that I net.

Up ahead, on the Medulla Sea of Rocks
are *raising a stink* and *sold down the river*
sunning, knowing they are safe.
They even sing to me; they wink.

In their hands are *many things* and *is evident*
offered like magic vials, like kisses
they blow to me in a cloud of bubbles.
They are shameless with smiles.

I motor past waving reeds and into a cove.
A few carp leer beside my rocking boat.
I'm shipwrecked in the left hemisphere,
swallowed by tangled seaweed.

I'm lost from *slub, haze,* or *shimmed,*
frizzle or *nubble* on the leeward side,
my ponderous tongue bumps on water,
unable to raise a voice.

Front of the Bus

On the bus trip, I sit so my students won't see
the thinning spot I can't cover with tint.
I know it glows like a burning bush
where the sun has fingered its way in.
From the back, laughter trumpets past
snippets of small talk weaving together
on a slow float forward. No one sits,
for the first time, where I can add
connections to this patchwork of teen talk.
Years ago, I sat on a bus behind Ms. K,
taskmaster of looming demands.
No one sat near her as she stared past
these same empty trees, heard
the same lumber of bus wheels.
Behind her back, we imitated how she
nodded off during the Hardy book panel,
boasted about prize-winning roses,
pronounced spelling's two l's like a w.
Yet we were her proud flock,
perched over our pens, thirsty for white paper
when she cannoned vocabulary in steady fire,
ready to guess a character's epiphany.
Once, delivering a book to her house, I found her
standing among her hundreds of roses,
sunlight haloing her luminous face
as she clipped me a fragrant handful,
tucked one in my thick, brown hair.
For the year I inherited her classroom,
I searched for her handouts, imprints
she left on the blackboard, but found her
only in my voice instructing students.
Without a protagonist to lead us,
we each take our seat at the front of the bus.
In the rearview mirror, a stranger stares
back, her face with its own story.

Control in the Classroom

Hold up your hand for silence.
Take the room like a joystick.
Don't let those mice leave the box.

Be careful with permission.
Chew words before offering
them like chocolate bullets.

Take notes. You'll need to verify
that cooperative learning produces
better test scores for the state.

The loners finish early, quietly
read *Clockwork Orange* instead
of messaging text or beating Tetra.

While they're listening, talk
fast, reel them, coax them.
Don't get caught holding

a wet line, an empty pen,
a mouse's chewed tail.
The silence should call for a knife.

A Bulletin from Your Principal

We will have PDC sessions during PLC on Nov 1 (groups A and B) and Nov 26 (groups C and D) in Room 224 to talk about ACT, SAT, NAEP, EOC, AP, and AP options. Olivia Williams from the RPDC at UMKC will be presenting DOK during the PDC time of PLC, and we'll have breakout sessions to work on Benchmarks* for state testing.

*

bench mark: a mark on a permanent object
☐ b: something that serves as a standard by which others may be measured or judged
☐ c: a standardized problem or test that serves as a basis for evaluation or comparison

Grading

We've watched
the moon sag
into tomorrow,
ready to set down
our pens.

They argued
their case,
we ours—
more detail,
another example,
better verbs.

We've stroked
our chins, pulled
our earlobes,
shifted our feet.

Ink glides its
well-oiled
ball bearings,
eager to praise
a phrase,
to find
a moment
of thought.

The Madeline Hunter Model

Lesson Date – Monday.   No. of Students – 188 total in a day
Room Number – 202, 302, 117   Lesson – Allusions and Research
Teacher's Name – Any English Teacher

What is the lesson objective: To ascertain Cultural Literacy through
Recognition of Allusions and how they appear in literature, and history

Student Anticipatory Set:
        If we all make good grades on the test, can we stop working?

Teacher Anticipatory Set:
        Oral Discussion: Let's see how many of these allusions you already
know. [Teacher is to make no assumptions as students will have different
backgrounds.]

Teaching/instructional Process:
        The teacher provides common literary allusions to ascertain
students' cultural literacy from reading, background exposure, former
study, and interacting with life.

Guided Practice: I'm going to give you examples of literary allusions,
and let's see which ones you already know before we look some of them
up to widen our background experience.

[Following are the allusions and the answers the students gave]

Lucifer – a cat in Cinderella
Iago – the bird in Aladdin
Sirens – what's on police cars
Helen of Troy – she makes hair dryers
Mercury – the stuff in thermometers—no wait, the guy who delivers flowers
Agamemnon – he was the king of some country in the Middle East
John Lennon – he invented those little round glasses
Benjamin Franklin – invented electricity
William Tell – had an apple shot off his head
Michelangelo – A Ninja Turtle
Red Queen – a chess piece or maybe a famous drag queen

Closure: I think we've seen that many of you recognize modern pop culture icons and advertising names connected to famous allusions in history and literature.

Independent Practice:

Now, we'll all go to the library to look up the original source of these allusions, and in doing so, perhaps know why an advertiser chose them or why these characters have these names.

Alumni Gather for the K-12 Centennial

In the gym, I sing the fight song as cheerleaders
build pyramids and flip into splits. I wander past tables
of faded ribbons, chipped megaphones, and a Memory Book for sale.

Over old football programs and yearbooks, alumni spill stories.
My cousin Larry recaptures his touchdown pass. Linda recounts
the night seniors hoisted the Zarda cow to the roof.

The elementary-school tables remind me of days we sat
as tidy as shelved cans, composing on thick-lined paper
or shaping clay vases and hand turkeys for our mothers.

Chapel Elementary has strung a clothesline of photos:
Teddy holding his trophy, Ben as Superman, Nedra slack jawed
in a bus seat, teachers waving from vacation at the Eiffel Tower.

I recognize a young Miss Penny, long before the Miss Penny
of black witch shoes stomped down aisles. Through windows,
the punished watched ropes turn, softballs sail over mitts.

Her stick slapped the blackboard and sent us back to maps
or division. The new kid that year, I let Cindy wrap a tetherball
above my reach every day to avoid waiting for a team, a turn, a place.

Linda shakes me back to Ouija-board parties, Big Boy fries,
the paper wad fight after days of *Silas Marner*. The band starts
the school song. I raise someone's pom-poms and sing.

At The Teacher Retirement Party

For years, I brought them cookies, lilacs;
they gave me fudge, bulbs, visited
after the appendectomy. I bought
their Tupperware®, sampled their baklava,
held their babies, who grew up in snapshots.
Now, we sip Merlot around Sarah's fireplace,
admiring pine wreaths. Sharon says, *The stock market
has been good to us this year*. Ann recalls Jim's
exploding pen, hall streakers, and Sally chuckles
over the class that duct-taped Mark to the wall.
We shift to the election, and Darlene calls
a candidate a *fool*. I take a sip. Judy announces,
She voted for him, and points at me. The room inhales
to silence. I shrug as sweat dampens my sweater.
My head fills with shell rush. A spark pops.
A shifting log thuds against the grate.
Someone suggests the artichoke dip. They realign
in the kitchen to admire new Silestone® counters,
talk about their Alaskan cruises. I feed Bruce
a dog biscuit, pretend an interest
in the still life hanging on the wall.

Regrets: *Final Exam*

1. Solve: $2X \div (Y\sqrt{} - \text{running across the boulevard}) =$
   Show Proof

2. Regret: (Choose the best answer)
   A. choosing in darkness the navy blazer with black shoes
   B. finding wood roach in the bottom of the teacup
   C. stepping barefoot where the copperhead sunned
   D. biting down on a hidden olive pit

3. Pick one of the following and explain the cause or the result:
   A. waving at Mick Jagger instead of a soldier going to war
   B. waking up under a tangle of limbs exhaling J&B
   C. looking at the question as if it were a dice roll, death mask, Freddie
   D. standing like a tumbler's glassy slurry in the arena bathroom line

4. Design a web site using only the photo by the lake, the unworn diamond, the wine stain, the contact in the toilet, a broken door handle and the dropped ball.

5. Camera: not shooting ::
   A. leaving home: coming back
   B. rounding up a dozen sheep: growing too old to run
   C. backseat: naked at the lake
   D. condom: stop!

6. Link all of the following and discuss the long-term effects: sunburns, disturbing the monarch's path, the cave, staring into the sun.

Teaching 5   Collage   Maryfrances Wagner

Notes

In Lord of the Flies by William Golding, a plane filled with British choir boys crashes on a deserted island. The pilot dead, the boys create their own democracy with rules. In time, the antagonist, Jack, wants to eat more than fruit and decides he will kill a wild pig with sharpened sticks. Some of the boys join his tribe. After their first kill and everyone eats meat, the society they have created starts breaking down. Fear of an unknown beast, each other, and a pig's head on a stick as a sacrifice drives the younger boys to protection from Jack's tribe where cruelty thrives, and deaths occur. Democracy and order break down when the boys stop following the rules they created.

A Separate Peace by John Knowles is a rite of passage story set during World War II at a boy's prep school. Finny, the all-star athlete, falls from a tree that Gene, his best friend, may have jiggled to cause the fall. It's a story of loss of innocence, wrestling with one's self, and realization.

"The Sophomores Study Julius Caesar" and "My Sophomores View the Eclipse" allude to characters, events, and lines from William Shakespeare's *Julius Caesar*, a play commonly read in Sophomore English.

The Detention Suite. I named this section Detention Suite because our school district had what they called Steps when students broke rules or caused discipline problems. They received a warning for their first time, and after that they went to all-day in-school suspensions followed by out of school suspensions as the infractions added up. I didn't think that taking students out of class solved the problem, so instead, I gave them after-school detention they served with me, and most of the time, it was only the two of us sitting in my classroom. They were supposed to work on their homework, but much of the time, they ended up telling me their story.

Maryfrances Wagner's newest books are *The Immigrants' New Camera, Solving for X*, and a reissue of *Red Silk*. She co-edits *I-70 Review*, serves as president of The Writers Place board and programming chair, was 2020 Missouri Individual Artist of the Year, and was Missouri's 6th Poet Laureate 2021-2023. *Red Silk* won the Thorpe Menn book award and was first runner up in the Eric Hoffer Legacy Award 2024 (reissued in 2023) and Short Listed for the Grand Prize Poetry. Poems have appeared in *New Letters, Midwest Quarterly, Laurel Review, American Journal of Poetry, Poetry East, Voices in Italian Americana, Main Street Rag, Rattle, Unsettling America: An Anthology of Contemporary Multicultural Poetry* (Penguin), *Literature Across Cultures* (Pearson/Longman), et. al. She is the granddaughter of four Italian Immigrants. She has taught workshops for students of all ages, taught high school writing and literature classes, served as department chair, district coordinator for English, was adjunct faculty at UMKC teaching undergraduate and graduate classes for over twenty years, and was the coordinator for the High School College Program at UMKC where she mentored teachers teaching college classes off campus, organized in-service training, served on the composition committee, and taught academic writing at the graduate level.

www.ingramcontent.com/pod-product-compliance
Lightning Source LLC
Chambersburg PA
CBHW030511130626
46549CB00007B/2941